The Other Side

The Other Side

THE POETRY OF NANA
DADZIE GHANSAH

• • •

Nana Dadzie Ghansah

Copyright © 2016 Nana Dadzie Ghansah
All rights reserved.

ISBN: 0998192902
ISBN 13: 9780998192901
Library of Congress Control Number: 2016917564
Nana Dadzie Ghansah, Lexington, KY

In everyone's life, at some time, our inner fire goes out. It is then burst into flame by an encounter with another human being. We should all be thankful for those people who rekindle the inner spirit.

—Albert Schweitzer

Dedicated to all who saw it, even though I did not. Thank you so much.

Prologue
• • •

Prologue

The Other Side

• • •

With longing I stare
At the other side;
How can I still bear
This great divide?
On my knees I fall,
A prayer on my lips;
For change I call—
Will joy my pain eclipse?
Then hope is distant;
My courage flees.
The pain is persistent;
My spirit pleads.
Will my day ever come?
Or will I to despair succumb?

Love, Lust, and Broken Hearts

...

Interlude

• • •

HER HANDS WERE CLASPED TOGETHER as if to reassure herself. The tumor made her forgetful, but he filled in the blanks seamlessly. There was care in his eyes. I looked at them—an older couple. I asked how long they'd been married. "Sixty years." Her face lit up. They had gotten married a day in June those many years ago. She said it was on his birthday. He said that was the only day he could get off. He reached out his hands. She unclasped hers and grabbed his. Something had suddenly replaced the fear and worry in her eyes. They were full of something delicate and tender…I think I saw tears…and love…lots of love.

The Art of Love

•••

You say you want my heart;
It's broken here and there,
Held together by an art
Unpracticed and quite rare.

A skill not difficult to acquire—
The desire one must have;
A skill one can most admire,
To the soul can be a salve.

Reception leads to a smile,
A day, a night, both bright.
One's worth goes a long mile;
There's nothing but light.

Giving it fills the soul—
A satisfaction unending.
The being at once is whole
From blessings cascading.

An ancient art indeed—
Love is the name it got.
Shown in word and deed,
It cannot be bought.

So if my heart you desire,
The art of love do learn.
Together we can aspire
Its intricacies to discern.

Symphony of the Hips

. . .

Alone at the bar she stood,
Regal and looking so good.
This rose I've got to get—
Snatch her in my net.
To the bar I made my way.
Time for the player to play.

Across from her I stood,
Dumb like a piece of wood.
Stricken by her looks,
A beauty for the books.
All I could was admire
An elegance that was afire.

Her eyes had a shine—
Could swear they were divine.
The gracious rise of her nose,
Just as confident as her pose.
Above red lips so full,
Like stuffed with tender wool.

A neck that gracefully flowed
Into a chest that was bestowed

By a pair ever perfect
In slope, firm and erect,
Adorned a trunk on a waist
Slim, dainty, and well placed.

The flare of her hips,
Those curves, those dips,
The back, that mound,
The hill, so round
On legs tapering down,
Long, lithe, and brown.

Spellbound did I stand,
All words from me banned
As she turned and walked away
Still holding me in her sway.
From her beauty subdued,
I stood there and stewed.

It's been quite a while,
The memory still fertile.
Each time I close my eyes,
I hear the fall and rise
Of the symphony of her hips—
The bounce, the zips, the flips.

Joy

• • •

Let me give you joy,
Be your boy toy.
Let yourself enjoy
Me as passion's envoy.
Remember us in Hanoi?
Sailing on the Viceroy?
My presence did not annoy;
Your guiles you did deploy,
My affection to employ,
All resistance to destroy.
In that you were not coy.
So take me in like the horse in Troy,
With our bodies merged into an alloy.
We'll once again scream, "Ahoy!"

Bang! Bang!

. . .

She stared down at him,
No mercy in her eyes.
His chances were slim—
She didn't have anything nice,
Only a loaded gun
Pointed at his heart.
Mercy—there'll be none.
Time for him to depart,
For his cruelty to cease,
For her to find her peace.
Bang!
Bang!

To the Woman

• • •

The weaker sex she is not.
Don't try to tie her in a knot!
The fairer one she is for sure.
What a being! What allure!
In her womb a life forms;
From her loins the life storms.
A mother dearest is gold,
For she keeps away the cold.
As a wife she is the buttress,
To a man forever the fortress.
As a sister, that ear
For everything that's dear.
As a friend, that shoulder
For tears never gets older.
As a leader, that vision,
A better life they envision;
They make this world better,
Our lives all so sweeter,
Beautiful, radiant, lovely,
Gorgeous, graceful, bubbly.

Kuukua, Ewurabena, Ama,
Betty, Angela, and Oduma:
Without you this life is gray;
Without you we go astray.

My Muse

•••

My muse, my muse,
Please excuse,
'Cause I need your cues,
My rhymes to fuse.
It's all a ruse;
Then you give the clues
From which I choose
The flows and hues.
When I sing the blues,
Kneeling in the pews,
You bring me the news
That makes me cruise.
I do not abuse
Or try to misuse,
So do not confuse
My intentions or lose
Me and refuse
My love's ooze.
Forever transfuse
Me with the brews
Of your love's dews,
So I can infuse
My rhymes with your juice.

Whispers of Her Feet

• • •

I sing of days gone by,
Hours lost in time's eye
When in love's good terms I was.
Caught up in her mighty claws,
She showered me with graces,
Adored me with her gazes.
My tunes are of times
When blissful chimes
Made hearts melt,
And desire was felt
For that tender touch
That said so much.
Kisses wet and soft,
They carried one aloft
Into love's sensuous gasp,
Holding tight in her clasp.
Now through the sheen of my sorrow,
The haze of a dark tomorrow,
I stretch my arm to touch
Just a bit, not much,
Of the hem of love's long gown,
Hoping my sorrow to drown.

Alas, all I can hear
To my ears not dear
Are whispers of her feet,
Swift and sure on the street
As they recede into the night,
Leaving me to my plight.

O Lovely and Graceful One

• • •

Balanced on her head,
The pot had found a bed.
With dignity the load she bore.
With grace one would adore,
The water sloshed around—
Sounds of her homebound.
Graceful, dark, and tall,
She made most men stall.

He's had his eye on her,
For emotions she did stir.
Her beauty was beyond
Any that had ever dawned.
She made his heart go soft,
His spirits up and aloft;
Talk to her he must,
Before he turned to dust.

O lovely and graceful one,
Like you there is none.
A word with you to share
Has always been my dare.
I mounted courage today,

So speak to me, I do pray.
Then my heart you would warm;
Calm would you bring to the storm.

O how gracious of you!
For kindness you are due.
Then your words are sweet,
And willing ears they meet.
For many a day I saw
You look at me from yore,
And oft did I wonder;
Your intentions did I ponder.

O lovely and graceful one,
Your beauty is second to none,
I never wished to scare,
To cause fear with my stare;
Forgive me if I did.
My shame I cannot rid.
Away, forever, and gone
I'll be, if you wish, by morn.

O ye of good intention,
Of fleeing make no mention.
Your words are indeed noble,
And of action you seem able.
However, home I must.
You understand, I trust.
This load to deliver,
For it is needed ever.

O lovely and graceful one,
Beauty as radiant as the sun,

My inconsideration please forgive;
Your presence is to me addictive—
Made me your duties to overlook;
Too much of your time I took.
Can I your load bear—
You, the toil to spare?

A man with a helpful heart,
Your demand must I thwart.
My load is mine to bear,
With none other to share.
Every morn, to the well I haste;
Not a minute do I waste.
If perchance you are nigh,
My dear heart shall not sigh.

O lovely and graceful one,
Your presence I cannot shun.
By the well in the morn will I be,
You in your radiance to see.
Now to your duties speed;
Of me take no more heed,
For in my heart is joy awake,
Newly alive for its sake.

As he watched her walk away,
In his heart he did pray:
Life, another day to live,
So his heart he could give
To beauty and grace so deep
That out of her did it seep
And light up her soul,
Making her so whole.

Together
• • •

On their backs they both lay,
The time as if to slay.
At the ceiling they gazed,
Joyous and amazed
At where they had been
And what it could mean
To two people in each other
In a world without a bother.
Their breaths came out in sharp, short bursts,
For into a sea of ecstasy they had been thrust.
The sweat on their bodies did glisten;
There was passion if you could listen.
She turned toward him
In the light that was dim,
Wrapped her arms around his nakedness,
Soaking her warmth in his manliness.
He looked lovingly in her eyes,
The feeling reaching new highs,
Then kissed her with all passion.
His need he could not ration.
She moaned and softly arched.
Her back, even as he marched
With her again into potential bliss.

Their lips locked together in a kiss;
Their rhythmic motion a choreographed dance,
The unheard music leading them in a trance.
Two souls together as one
In a brew of love perfectly done.
The climax, an explosion
Of their pent-up emotion.
As her screams pierced the air,
Laying all what was inside bare,
Her nails dug into his warm skin;
Her toes curled into a spin.
As his embrace tightened,
So was his joy heightened.
Their breaths became short, sharp bursts,
For into ecstasy they had been thrust.

The Beauty Behind

• • •

Don't leave your beauty behind,
O ye of shapely curves!
Then to fall it seems inclined
That one sure observes.
It rolls and twirls with every step.
Undulating to its own beat,
It sings and chants with spirit and pep—
A treat I think is sweet.
Keep walking, O my shapely one;
Those buns I do adore.
Keep moving that curvaceous ton;
I'll help if you are sore.
I'll watch them with all my love,
Hover over them from above.

The Other

• • •

I yearn for your touch,
Your sweet and soft caress.
To your memories I clutch
Even when her body I possess.
I hold her but feel your warmth.
I look at her but see your face.
She is south, but you are north,
In your very special place.
My longing for you will not stop.
It into desire for her I cannot morph;
My tears for you dare not drop,
For then she'll surely wipe them off.
If she does, I cannot withstand
The wish that it was your hand.

Do you still yearn for her touch?
Her sweet and gentle caress?
To what memories do you clutch?
Whose body do you possess?
Do you still feel her warmth
And see her face?
Now she is definitely south,
In a not-so-special place.

Can your pain into desire morph?
Do your tears dare drop?
I'll not wipe them off.
You do not have to withstand
The thought that it's my hand.

Kay

• • •

Her screen name was Kay.
I wrote, "Let's play."
She sent a cool pic.
I thought she was slick.
The conversations were cyber,
The hours together hyper.
We lol'ed to jokes
And sent each other pokes.
We set our emotions afire,
Our need for each other dire.
We planned one day to meet
So as our longing to defeat.

And so I stood that day
Behind the door like a stray.
My heart pounded fast
As the bell I rang at last.
When I heard the clicks,
My feet felt like bricks.
Slowly, the door opened.
Wil I be chastened?
And then our eyes did meet.
Through me I felt the heat.

The beauty in the door
I surely could adore.

The Ride

• • •

Her name was Akosua.
She hailed from Bosua.
Smiling did she greet
And walked me to my seat.
Into plush leather I settled.
In total comfort I nestled.
As she came closer to me,
Her hip touched my knee.
She looked me in the eyes,
And with a sweet guise,
Her fingers strummed my face
At a slow and steady pace.
Then in a voice all smooth and silky,
She said these words all so milky,
"Your pleasure is my duty,
So enjoy the ride, my cutie!"
Eyes closed as fingers strummed,
I sighed as I finally succumbed.

Valentine

• • •

Sweet, sweet Clementine
Will you be my Valentine?
Let our two hearts entwine
Like the branches of a vine.
Do not my passion malign,
Nor my affection decline.
Let me your love enshrine
In this heart that is thine.
Tingles go down my spine
At your beauty so divine.
You are like red roses fine.
Your looks do style define.
So let me pick you up at nine.
Thus you and I can dine
On caviar, oysters, and wine
By the river at the Tyne,
And in the moon's glowing shine,
On my knees I'll sing the line,
"Baby, baby, please be mine!"

Shadows of My Hopes

• • •

The setting sun,
From silky yellow spun,
Did your shadow cast
Into the waters that ran past,
Where I stood quite unsure
And dumbstruck by your allure.
As the cascading drops from the fall
Picked up your beauty in a squall,
I stood alone on the other side,
Your timeless beauty in my eye.
I hesitated while he did not.
So there I stood in afterthought.
As the fairness of your sight
Receded into the moonlight,
The billowing cloud of my regret
Enveloped me like cold sweat.
I come back every year.
From that I never veer,
Hoping in the yellow moonlight,
Casting your shadow all bright,

The Other Side

Your beauty again to behold,
And get my soul consoled.
Alas, as the water falls down the slopes,
All I see are just shadows of my hopes.

The Offer

• • •

I will make you scream,
Make you call my name,
Fulfill your wildest dream.
You won't be the same.
See this body of mine?
It can all be yours,
These curves, so fine,
Much pleasure ensures.
Are you full of worry?
A heart filled with care?
You won't be sorry
Into these arms to dare.
So out with the wallet, and pay my fee.
My love is the best but is sure not free!

The Chaos in Your Eyes

• • •

I get lost
In the chaos in your eyes,
Tossed
Into a sea of my demise.
The attraction is strong
From emotion that's raw.
I am strung along,
Powerless and in awe.
You hold me in a trance,
Hypnotized and enslaved.
I succumb to your romance,
Decadent and depraved,
As I see colors forceful and bold
Between lines that slowly unfold.

Come Back to Me

• • •

He:
What can I do without you?
Apparently nothing!
I never had a clue
That you are my everything.
You made it bearable,
This crazy journey.
The loneliness is terrible.
I'm losing this tourney.
I go through the motions,
Master of pretense,
Dealing with emotions,
Of which one is regret.
Come back, and make things right!
Come back, and I'll hold you tight.

She:
Time has removed the scales
That covered my eyes.
My soul suffered from the tales
Of your numerous lies.
You left me for her,
Turned your back on me.

She you did prefer.
You never heard my plea.
Then when it felt the bleakest,
He walked into my life.
He's taken me from the lowest
To love and no strife.
I'll stay with him, for he made it right!
I'll stay with him, for he holds me tight!

This Thing Called Life...and Death
...

Interlude

• • •

AND THEN HE TOOK ME to the top of the mountain and said, "Visualize a world with no strife!" So I closed my eyes, and that is when I saw the chasm—a great chasm it was indeed—on one side was much prosperity and abundance and on the other much need, hunger, and suffering.

I opened my eyes and asked him, "I see a great chasm. How can I visualize no strife with such a great chasm?"

He looked at me, smiled, and said, "Fill the chasm!"

So I asked, "With what?"

He said, "With *empathy*."

To Dad

• • •

Like sunset over the Volta,
The end set on your story,
Our lives are but a delta
In the flow of your glory.
Words of wisdom remembered,
Acts of integrity unmatched,
Patient, thoughtful, kindhearted—
You stood for the right, unabashed.
Each year on this day,
Since you left us in tears,
We yearn these words to say.
Hope you hear them upstairs.
A father you were in every sense.
Thank you for lessons so immense.

Vacant

• • •

I was always your bird
Flying into the heavens,
For you always spurred
Me with your lessons.
But now at me you stare
With a look that is bare
And vacant.

You gave me your strength,
Filled me with your courage.
From you I took the breath.
You stayed forever my sage,
But now at me you stare
With a look that is bare
And vacant.

Remember the first tooth?
The very first step I took?
How you sought to soothe
When strife my life shook?
But now at me you stare
With a look that is bare
And vacant.

The games and pranks,
Camping and fishing,
I'm full of thanks
And still wishing
That you won't stare
With a look that's bare
And vacant.

I can't stop the tears.
Memories roll around;
I can't quell my fears;
They surely abound.
For now you stare
With a look that's bare
And vacant.

I'll cherish the moments,
Treasure your love,
Which has no opponents
And wraps me like a glove.
So though you stare
With a look that's bare,
My heart is not
Vacant.

The Voices

• • •

The voices, those voices,
Speaking words, saying things—
The flow is incessant
The terror is constant
Cannot tell a soul what I know;
The secrets weigh on my soul.
How can I hope to grow,
Toiling in this terrible role?
The demands atrocious,
Unimaginable, stomach churning.
My fear capacious,
In my corner, turning, yearning.
Another life I cannot take,
A position I cannot forsake.

Before Dawn

• • •

The night is darkest before dawn.
As I wait for the hour to strike,
My soul is all forlorn
As the fear and dread spike.

I seek the embrace of death,
An end to my sorrow.
He comes to take my breath
Before a new tomorrow.

I'll miss the ones I love;
Their embrace I most treasure,
Though now I wear the glove
Of life's deep displeasure.

As his cold fingers reach
My spirit, weary and tired,
I close my eyes and beseech
By the rebirth to be inspired.

He Will Prevail

• • •

Death, O death!
Be not so sure
That after his last breath,
You will him lure
Along that dark and lonely trip
To the land of endless night,
Into your cold, hard grip
From which there's no flight.
Wallow not in your pride
If before you he does appear,
For he shows not to abide;
He comes to conquer fear.
Death! Over you he will prevail!
Death! Eternal life we will hail.

Hate

• • •

Hate—
Does that word emanate
From places innate,
Only to dissipate
When we open the gate?

Hate,
Are you irate
That I have a trait
That you underrate
And wish to segregate?

Hate,
When I menstruate
Instead of ejaculate,
Does it negate
My right to adjudicate?

Hate,
Do I have a mate
That you won't date,
So mandate
Me a loveless fate?

Hate,
Does your deity negate
The belief of others, castigate
As you lay prostrate
Or read your Vulgate?

Hate,
Can we debate,
Or even deflate,
Try to placate
This sorry state?

Wishes

• • •

I wished upon a star
In the blue sky afar
My jewels a tad to enhance;
Woe but to me did advance.
A twelve-inch pianist and a song,
A wish gone all wrong.

I called upon the gods,
Hoping but for nods.
For a million bucks my way
On my knees I did pray.
Woe but me now do follow
A million ducks in my sorrow.

I yearn for a pretty wife
With which to share this life.
Endowed with a big butt,
Shapely, round, and hot.
Woe, but do I dare ask
What may I unmask?

A wish is sure a horse—
For the beggar, the source

Of that ride to dreams,
To a place where all seems
Possible, true, and real,
Till reality's bells peal.

Hooves of Time

• • •

Ta-thump, ta-thump, ta-thump,
I hear the hooves of time—
A noise not at all sublime—
Crashing in the distance,
To my thoughts a hindrance,
A whisper once upon a time,
Now clearer than a chime,
Creeping closer and closer,
Sounding bolder and bolder.
I feel the need to hurry,
To my destination to scurry.

Ta-thump, ta-thump, ta-thump,
I fear the hooves of time—
A noise at all not sublime.
Tidings of the end they bear,
News to my ears not dear.
So through the light of days,
Dim as the sun with no rays,
To my destination I make haste.
Not a moment do I waste
To be ready for the date
With time at the gate.

Tired

• • •

Slowly it comes over you,
Covering like morning dew.
The steps do get heavier,
Thought of the next scarier.
The eyes sure do droop
Like the roof of an old coop.
A back that was straight
Bends from this fate.
A smog covers the mind,
Holding it in a tight bind.
Such a state holds sway
Over one after a long day.
Then is one mentally uninspired,
For the being is physically tired.

Watch Me

...

Watch me slanging;
White rocks I'm dealing.
Lots of paper making,
Starving mouths feeding—
That's right!

Watch me rolling,
In the E55 speeding.
Beside me Cutie is lounging,
All eyes on me watching
How we do!

Watch me balling,
The fifties and hundreds spending.
Cognac and bubbly flowing,
The ice on my wrist blinging.
I'm fly!

Watch me running,
The popo after me chasing.
Gunfire over all ringing,
Bullets around me flying.
Life sucks!

Watch me wailing—
Twenty years could be slamming.
Behind bars will be chilling,
Hardest time doing.
I'm done!

Watch me snitching,
About the deals telling.
The feds sure are listening;
I call it negotiating.
What's up!

See me swinging,
Belt around my neck hanging.
Hard life slowly fading,
My chapter sure is ending.
That's all!

Silence

• • •

I call out your name;
Deep silence stares.
I look for the flame;
There are no flares.
Do you hear me?
I'm out here waiting.
Do you hear my plea?
The quiet is grating.
Why did you leave?
Into the void flee?
For your loss I grieve,
Wishing to be with thee.
Only deep silence stares
At a flame without flares.

But for Grace

• • •

As the sun set on his life,
One of long days and cold nights,
In his heart was no strife,
For on eternity he had his sights.
On a face marred by pits of pain
So deep that they hid his tears,
You could swear a smile did reign
And not a hint of any fears,
For Grace held his hands,
Her warm presence ever near;
For Grace warmed the sands
Of time, so they were dear.
But for Grace, a life unknown.
But for Grace, a death alone.

The Battery Is in the Lord

• • •

I had a little roadster;
The Lord was its name.
It was a real speedster,
On the road its reign.
Took it for a spin one day,
With the white top down,
Foot on the gas all the way,
Headed out of town.

A radar detector is a must;
Then cops on the road abound.
I reached out mine to adjust,
But a dead screen I found.
I pulled over to the side
With the device to fiddle.
I opened it and sighed—
No battery in the cradle!

Disappointed, I headed back,
Another battery to get.
Sadness did my soul attack
And regret my spirit beset.
Then a glint caught my eye

On the floor of the car.
The brakes I did apply,
For I had seen a star.

I yelled out as my spirits soared,
"The battery is in the Lord."

Sam the Man

• • •

I am Sam the Man.
My might over centuries span,
Most powerful of them all;
Before me they all fall.
My will reaches far and wide;
From it no one can hide.
Mighty spirits cook the brew
Into which my wishes they hew.
Poured into spells fast and true,
They are always on point and cue.
Spells to kill,
Spells to chill
Those aloof enough
My reach to rebuff;
Spells to heal,
Spells to steal
Your soul if I must,
And that is not unjust;
Spells to make weak
All before me meek,
For after your manhood I come
To make you just another bum.
So stay out of my way;

Jump out of the fray,
For I am Sam the Man,
The *strongest* in the *clan*.

Shell

• • •

Are you but a shell
Of what you used to be?
Life been a living hell,
Not a chance or a plea?

Has your strength deserted you,
Like Samson without hair?
Do you feel the pending dew
Of the end in the air?

Do your bones moan and creek
Like an old chair in the attic?
Do your eyes search and seek
But to see the little tick?

A shell you're not,
For you have a spirit.
Stand tall you ought,
For there's still life in it.

Flood of Memories

• • •

Alas it was time,
The moment prime,
The last of the boxes to open,
Being last a good omen.
Still apprehension filled his heart;
From it he could not depart.
The unknown a dim place,
Not known to be full of grace.
Like the dimly lit room,
So full of gloom,
He found himself in
Seeking the hidden within.
As he flipped the lid open,
His whole being hoping,
Old pictures stared back at him,
Faint in outline and dim.
Unable to clearly perceive
The secrets they might conceive
The box to the window he carried,
His step there a little hurried.
As he pulled the curtains apart,
His heart to pound did start,

For into the room flooded
Memories that haunted.

Shackles

• • •

As he took the baby in his arms,
The pride in his eyes
Washed over her like charms
From a wizard's guise.
He looked around the cage
Made of concrete and metal
And felt inside the rage
That would not settle.
The chance to hold her
Was unexpected and warm.
The experience did spur
Him to wish for the norm.
He looked up at the clock;
His time was up.
Suddenly he took stock,
And staring into the cup
That was his life,
A tear fell from sad eyes,
Fanning the strife
That fed into his sighs.
Before he handed her over,
On her cheek he placed a kiss.
His heart sank lower

Over chances he would forever miss
As they led him shuffling away,
Shackles, cuffs, and all,
He promised to himself to pray
For a chance to be tall,
As only a father can.

A Mother's Lament

• • •

This flag that I hug
Is cold, unlike his embrace.
It cannot heal the tug
On my heart or replace
Him and what he meant.
My love, my only son,
My being does lament
For a youth that is done.
The war that took your life
Spilled the love of a mother.
Pain that cuts like a knife,
Stifling, makes me smother.
You went to war to fight for our peace,
Except I lost you, and my hurt won't ease.

The Song

• • •

Inspired by Farrah and dedicated to all breast-cancer survivors

Lying down, she closed her eyes,
Ready to let her sad soul fly.
She had no more strength to rise,
Even a breath from her soul to ply.
Then she heard the sweetest song,
Full of joy, cheer, and hope;
Made her doleful heart long
For strength and pep to cope.
She opened her eyes to look
From where the sweet song flowed.
Then, with surprise, her being shook,
For to her soul the song she owed—
A sweet song of having survived,
From cancer the victory deprived.

Tears came flowing down
With memories of days of pain.
Once fear was her crown,
For the disease in her did reign.
Then sliced the surgeon's knife,
Removing what once nurtured,

All in a bid to preserve a life
From errant cells tortured.
Now she felt unwanted and haunted,
Ashamed of who she'd become.
Lo! Suddenly to sing she wanted
Of what her soul had overcome—
A sweet song of having survived,
From cancer the victory deprived.

A stranger stole her light,
Left her tapping in the dark.
In her was hardly any fight.
She yearned to find a spark.
From the scary world she hid,
Afraid to venture out.
She couldn't see herself amid
The bustle of out and about,
Except now she had a song
From her soul, with words that rang
To her to get up and be strong.
So with joy she got up and loudly sang
A sweet song of having survived,
From cancer the victory deprived.

Time
• •

If I could turn you back
For just a little while,
To take another crack
At things with a new style,
With that trend called hindsight
And wisdom, which is in vogue—
The chance to make wrongs right,
Mend hearts with one stroke,
Squeeze each single lemon
That grew on my tree
My own way, not the common.
So, time, do you hear me?
The silence was deep and thick,
Broken by tick, tock…and tick.

Through My Glasses

• • •

He asked for my glasses;
I handed them to him.
He starred at the scratches
And the scuffs on the rim.
The disdain in his blue eyes
Was evident, stark, and clear;
I hoped he'd think otherwise
When my life's view did appear.
He put my lowly glasses on
And soon was in my world.
On his face disbelief did dawn;
A mask of sadness unfurled.
He took my glasses quickly off,
Never more at another to scoff.

The Beauty of Life

• • •

Searing!
Tearing!
The pain
Insane.
Waves of it enveloping,
Over all developing.
Girl, push! Girl, push!
My tush! My tush!
Need some air—I gasp,
Need a hand—I grasp.

Will this ever stop
Before I finally drop?
Then a loud scream.
Is that but a dream?
Bloody, wet but warm,
Into the crook of an arm.
Full of pride,
Cannot hide
Pain as sharp as a knife,
Relief in the beauty of life.

Aren't We All Humanity

• • •

We stood looking at the carnage,
Frozen by the sight of the pillage
Of lives, chances, hopes, and dreams.
Beneath a cloud of unheard screams
With my sorrow totally unmasked,
I turned to him in tears and asked,
"Aren't we all humanity?"

"I like women; he likes men.
He faces the east; they say amen.
Chocolate skin, vanilla sheen,
She's up in years; he's just a teen.
Speaks Fante, sings in Russian,
Is an Eskimo, married a Persian.
Aren't we all humanity?"

Face thoughtful, he looked ahead,
Silent for a while, then finally said,
"Treat others like you would yourself—
A rule old and golden in itself.
Love and empathy it does breed,
For every faith must be the creed.
Else, I see humans but no humanity!"

A Strange Odor

• • •

An odor hangs in the air,
Pervasive and colorless.
Our senses it seeks to impair,
Its essence meaningless.
It's fed by the blood of lives,
Seeking but to matter
To him who to protect strives,
Yet ends up but a splatter.
It permeates a nation divided,
Unwilling to see humanity
In their values misguided,
Feeding into an insanity.
I smell death all over the land.
I smell death, unnatural and unkind.

Just Get Over It

• • •

You find it so unfair,
A target you seem to wear.
For to drive is but a gauntlet
Between blue lights and a bullet.
Makes you wonder if your color
Gives off a dark, punitive odor;
Yet all you seem to hear is,
Hey, just get over it!

The city streets you pound;
For a job you hound.
Yet not a door will open.
Then that color is a bad omen
That hovers like a bad spell
No one can ever dispel.
Don't ask, for you'll hear,
Hey, just get over it!

He likes the way you move.
Puts him in the groove.
His advances are a turnoff;
Those demands make you scoff.
The harassment you have to bear,

"For the career," you declare.
Think you'll find any pity?
Hey, just get over it!

Don't commit a crime,
For then you'll do time
That is colored in severity
And darker in intensity.
For justice in this land
Is not color-blind.
However, if you must,
Hey, just get over it!

When you call the shots,
You don't tie yourself in knots
Over how others live
Or even try to survive.
Empathy is a luxury,
Its practice a drudgery.
Much easier it is to say,
Hey, just get over it!

Don't Leave Me

• • •

The love that we share
Cascades down my soul.
Something so rare—
How it makes me whole!
It puts wings on my feet;
I fly around in glee.
Every sound of you, so sweet,
Sets me on a joyous spree.
With you, mountains are mere hurdles;
The valleys seem like tender dips.
All those life's battles
Appear as transient blips.
So don't leave me for his cold, dark arms.
Dear, don't fall for death's eternal charms.

In the Split Second

• • •

In the split second,
What do you see?
Do you see a human
Encased in a shell of fear?
Or do you only have the acumen
To see color as premier?

In that split second,
What do you feel?
Fear for your own
Or blinding hate?
Seek another tone,
Or is it too late?

In that split second,
What do you do?
Pull that trigger back
As bullets and life fly,
Or does your finger go slack,
As your biases you defy?

In that split second,
History flies by!

His life or your life,
Or maybe neither.
O what a strife,
In which color never takes breather!

Grandma's Tree

...

My dad was behind bars,
Doing life for taking a life.
My brother jacked cars;
It all ended with a knife.
Mum liked the pipe;
Haven't seen her in years.
I fit the stereotype,
Till Grandma allayed my fears.
She found the lump one day
As it crept here and there.
I watched her demise in dismay,
As she slowly lost her air.
Grandma, you'd be so proud of me.
Grandma, your sapling became a tree.

Dark Smoke

• • •

Dark smoke
Turns night into day.
Flashes evoke
The sun coming to stay.
Screams rip into the air,
Filled with drops of blood.
As limbs from bodies tear,
Horror flows like a flood.
They speak a language of pain
With words that sting,
Yet they seek to explain
That their way is king,
Causing suffering and destruction with impunity,
As a deity wonders about his Word and their humanity.

Pain

...

Four centuries of pain
Hit us like a hurricane.
They took our domain,
Our bodies they did detain
And with a long chain
Led us to fields of sugarcane
And treatment so inhumane
That some souls were slain.
Others suffered the cane,
Holding us all along in disdain.
From that they never refrain.
Makes one struggle to explain
How we possibly retain
Our ability to stay humane.
Wisdom and strength remain.
What we still need to regain
From the negative refrain,
So we can reattain
Lives blessed and sane.

The Crossing— the Departure

• • •

The ship danced in the water
Even as the shoreline receded.
Felt we were for the slaughter,
As voices over all pleaded.
From families we'd been torn,
Loved ones nothing but memories.
For the lives we had, we mourn;
Elapsed time felt like centuries.
In the future I see only pain;
My soul weeps at the thought.
Sanity I wonder if I can retain.
Fear holds my spirit distraught.
I miss my home; O woe is me!
Will I ever return, alive and free?

The Crossing—the Arrival

• • •

The sharp shaft of light
Pierced the darkness below,
Setting the gory sight
Of death and misery aglow.
I carried my heavy chains
With what strength I had,
Walking through lanes
With lifeless bodies clad.
Like cattle in a herd,
We shuffled to our fate
That fear in me spurred,
And I couldn't negate.
O fate, what pain do you hold?
O future, how will you unfold?

The Whip

• • •

The whip cracks,
Cutting through air.
His back it smacks;
Pain is his fare.
In the fog of blood and tears,
Memories of a distant home;
The suffering that he wears
Adorns his soul like a dome.
Again and again it cracks,
The air a sea of misery;
Even as his body it racks,
In his soul reigns victory.
O whip, his body you may break!
O whip, his spirit you will not take!

The Cup

• • •

Lord, if it be your will,
Take this cup from me.
From it I've had my fill
Of pain, so hear my plea.
The burden sure is heavy,
Its color quite dark.
A toll it does levy
On the soul, a sad mark.
See me for my content,
Not for this aphotic cup.
Hear me as I lament;
My soul does look up.
Lord, if you take this cup away,
Will my soul be left in disarray?

The Melting Pot

• • •

He found red beads in the pot
On the other side of the pond—
Now in our minds but a blot,
Sent off into a bloody beyond.
He refilled it with paler beads,
Darker ones all chained and tied,
Other colors, other creeds,
Did in the pot also abide;
To blend the colors into one,
The pot on a flame he did set;
After a while he thought, "It's done!"
So a melt he rushed to get;
Alas, what in the pot dwelt
A mix of cultures, not a melt.

Don't Flinch

• • •

Don't flinch, my son, or you are dead;
Don't blink, my son, or it all ends.
Don't even move your head
Or try to make amends.
That blue finger is itchy
That rests on the trigger.
For you there is no pity,
Only from the gravedigger.
Your color is too dark;
To society you're just a menace.
You make a good mark,
And they don't even do penance.
Don't flinch when you see the lights;
Don't flinch or insist on your rights.

Dark and Lonely Places

• • •

I stand
At a dark and lonely place,
Lifeless without grace,
And all I see are the stars.
Will all my scars
As they hurtle down—
They cannot even drown
My sorry state
And change my fate.

I stand
At a dark and lonely place.
Misery is all I face,
And my tears,
Carrying my fears,
Crash to the ground
Without a sound,
Quiet and still—
Not a soul to thrill.

I stand
At a dark and lonely place,
And there is no trace

Of love and affection.
Life without is passion,
Too unsure, too afraid,
At the edges all frayed,
If asking is right
To redeem my plight.

I stand
At a dark and lonely place,
And for a morsel I chase,
My body racked by hunger,
Piercing my being like a dagger.
The cold burns to the bone;
From the false warmth I moan.
I shake, shiver, and tremble;
From the world not a grumble.

I stand
At a dark and lonely place,
Lifeless and without grace.
I look around and swear
That what I see is not rare,
For the place I stand,
Forever banned,
Reminds me of places,
Lots of former spaces
Where I stood before.

To Kobe

• • •

Last night you dropped sixty—
Sure makes the eyes misty.
The years have been twenty;
Dude, the points quite plenty.
Those rings—you have five;
Those memories will thrive.
You worked hard at the game;
Without you it's not the same.
You go out in style,
Highlights by the mile,
So even as the lights go out,
We all scream and shout
Mamba out!

To Phife Dawg

• • •

He was on point and always bolder,
Shooting rhymes like arrows from an archer.
A five-foot assassin but no less dopper—
With mad style he stepped off the frankfurter.
Most times he was a mean poem sayer,
Other times a cool studio conveyor.
Now Phife is off to somewhere better,
So send a telegram to tell your father
That he leaves us here a little bit bleaker;
Then without him we have no rhyme savior.

Dear Martin

• • •

Eighty-seven you would be,
If the world then had a plea.
Thirty-nine young and full of life
When the bullet tore like a knife.
The dreams you left behind—
We took them and enshrined
Them in our hearts and minds.
Though sometimes hate still blinds
To character but not to color,
Sadly making our senses duller
To the pain of the other.
Our hopes we cannot smother;
Your vision we cannot forget,
For then we stand to beget
Faithless despair instead of hope
That leads down a slippery slope
Into an abyss dark and cold,
Where we shall grow old
And yearn for what could have been
If we had kept your dream within.
So even as we remember,
We will in our spirits engender,
With faith as our theme,
The strength to dream.

To the Victims of the Earthquake

• • •

The day she shook
Was the day she took
All of them away,
Back into clay,
Leaving misery-stricken faces
And death in tight spaces.

Fingers claw to reach,
Voices that beseech
The light of passing days,
As all hope slowly decays,
Making sorrow mix with tears
And echoes of silent prayers.

To Prince

• • •

That Lady in the Red Corvette—
One Sexy MF she was.
Looks that made you never forget,
A body that caused a buzz
Said, "My name is Prince.
I Wanna Be Your Lover."
Looked at me with a wince,
Said, "No, go in The Holy River."

The Most Beautiful Girl in the World,
Decked in Diamonds and Pearls,
As a Sexy Dancer, she twirled,
Raspberry Beret off, showing those curls.
Said, "Money Don't Matter 2 Night
So come and let us Kiss."
For just a minute, I thought she might;
Just then came the hiss.

Said, "Let's Pretend we're Married."
"Get Off!" she said with a sneer.
My world she just totally buried,
Standing there in her Pink Cashmere.
I wanted to party like it's 1999

The Other Side

Over at Paisley Park with her,
With Peach, Cream, and wine;
Now that will never ever occur.

Betcha Golly Wow!
You did it without an apology;
I guess now you take that bow,
Leaving us your Musicology
As you walk into the Purple Rain.
We understand When Doves Cry,
It's surely to hide the pain
When those they love leave for the sky.

To Muhammad Ali

• • •

You were not afraid.
Oh no!
You?
Not a hint!
After you climbed into the ring,
The world you shocked
With swagger and a swing,
As you Liston rocked.
You were not afraid.
Oh no!
You?
Not a hint!

The name Cassius to bury in Clay,
As you as Ali awakened
Pride in a people carried away
In pain and misery abandoned.
You were not afraid.
Oh no!
You?
Not a hint!

When that conscience spoke,
An unjust war you opposed,
Shaking off the old yoke.
Even as fortunes decomposed,
You were not afraid.
Oh no!
You?
Not a hint!

When justice came one day,
In Manila you did thrill,
Rumbling in Zaire in a display
Showing you were not over the hill.
You were not afraid.
Oh no!
You?
Not a hint!

As disease the body beset,
Slowing that quick gait,
Strength faced the threat
From a spirit that stayed great.
Alas, death has made
Its claim on you.
Yet you are not afraid.
You?
Oh no!
Not a hint!

Then even death cannot gloat,
Its sting no match ever,

For like a butterfly you float
On in our memories forever.
So go in peace, champ;
A great legacy you leave behind.
Then you have left a stamp
Of courage in each fan's mind.
So we are not afraid.
Us?
Oh no!
Not a hint!

To That Wildcat

...

In defeat you stood tall,
Clawing like a crazy wildcat
For points, rebounds, and all.
With body, mind, and heart.
You gave it all each night,
Never holding back an inch.
A size that belied the might,
At no time did you flinch.
This morn hearts are sad,
In a nation that's all blue.
The season was not all bad;
Then together we all grew.
You've taught us to give it all;
You've taught us to stand tall.

Ghana on My Mind
• • •

Interlude

• • •

THE SOUNDS OF THE RAINDROPS on the roof sounded like a thousand drums at Abangye. One could smell the thunderstorm. The bolts of lightning streamed through the glass of the window. I stepped out onto the porch, and the sight and smell of the rain took me back. All of a sudden, I was a little boy again playing in the rain with abandon. I was home.

My Prayer for Ghana at Fifty-nine

• • •

Fifty-nine, a number,
Fifty-seven to remember.
As we broke the yoke and chains,
Osagyefo looked at the gains
And marched us into the oasis
With vigor and long paces.
Soon, a vision much maligned
Was to be undermined.
Beguiled and confused as we watched,
From coups to republics we hopped.
As into the desert we wandered,
Our great potential squandered.

God bless our homeland, Ghana;
Over us shower your manna.
Fill them with wisdom and courage
That we may finally all engage
Our strength and spirit as a nation,
Filled with zeal and motivation
To be great, mighty, and strong,
To the successes of history belong.

Radiant from the summit, a beacon,
Never again mediocrity to beckon,
So anoint us in this great endeavor
With your grace forever and ever.

Say No to Mediocrity

• • •

Ghana, once home of sanity,
Birthplace of African vitality,
Say no to mediocrity!
Avoid that lowly travesty;
Escape at high velocity
From that terrible commodity.
It creeps into our normality,
Spreads with steady alacrity,
Perverting our mentality
To accept bitter commonality.

When a brochure is an atrocity,
The wording a calamity—
When our very locality
Is lost in absurd territoriality—
And with amazing inanity,
A leader's very identity
Is lost in common triviality,
Yet when with surprising audacity,
Devoid of any morality,
The responsible with laxity
Avoid sight of our new reality
And the situation's gravity—
Haven't we sunken into depravity?

Ghana, once home of sanity,
Birthplace of African vitality,
Proud in our nationality,
Now wallows with porcine joviality
In the depths of mediocrity.

Mother Ghana's Fall

Mother Ghana sat on a wall;
Down she went to a great fall,
Shoved off by Bad Governance
Scoffed at by Total Ignorance.
Patriotism rushed to her side,
As Hope and Vision did guide.
They tried to put her together again,
So her place and integrity to regain.
Corruption kept getting in the way;
With Greed they totally held sway.
Indiscipline got invited too,
Settling on Mother like dew.
And then appeared Mediocrity,
Who thwarted plans with alacrity.

Patriotism toiled against all that.
Soon had Mother Ghana all pat,
Alas on looking up at the wall
Where Mother sat before her fall,
Neglect and Apathy held court,
Destroying the wall like a sport.
It stood askew, leaning to a side.
Bricks were missing, far and wide.

Patriotism sighed, feeling defeated,
Tearing up at how Mother was treated.
With Vision blurred and Hope gone,
He stood alone beside her forlorn,
Wondering if there was really any use
Over Mother Ghana's effort to effuse.

Where We Go Pass

• • •

Charley, life for here hard oo!
Man no dey see top koraa oo!
Go ask price for petrol
You go lose control!
Small food man go chop sef,
You hear price, den you bore sef.
People see dem light bill,
I swear dey want take pill.

Despite, money de dey chop,
Dubai wey de dey go nonstop.
Dumsor diɛ, e de be!
You no like—go burn sea!
Buses wey dey spray,
The money paa dey pay!
Small picture man take,
So so matter koti make.

Eish! Matter be dis!
Where we go pass
Come reach here?
E no be say I hear
Say e go be kɛkɛ?

Now, I swear, e hard kɛkɛ
Wey we dey suffer kɛkɛ,
November go come oo, kwɛ
We go go vote kɛkɛ.

Dear Alhaji

• • •

Alhaji,
Can I take this picture
Of this instant capture,
As you abuse your power
And over us tower?
Remember you are the servant
To a people quite observant,
So when you send the dogs out
To intimidate and spout clout,
Can we take that picture
Of that instant capture
So as to remember
Come next November?

From the Darkness

• • •

Like Vikings they came to plunder,
Leaving a carcass behind,
After tearing the nation asunder
And robbing us all blind.
From the summit they pushed
Our souls into a deep abyss;
Our spirits were ambushed,
Into a darkness with no bliss.
Yet from the Dumsor shall arise,
Spirits strong and resolved,
From all the pain ready and wise
Above all to get involved,
The torch to set alight again,
The summit in glory to reattain.

The Prophecy

• • •

And so spoke the Okomfo
From his holy shrine in Tafo:
"Three years ye shall wonder
How your leader doth blunder.
You shall in the dark stumble,
As light goes out like a bubble.
Into the mediocre you will sink,
From the ordinary will you drink.

"Come the fourth, he shall appear,
His image on buses loud and clear.
Outhouses shall be erected,
Hundreds at places selected.
Gifts will he generously hand out,
North and south and throughout.
The cities shall have light
To brighten up the night.

"Even them shall many, many ask,
Why he doth now the good unmask?
Others shall him loud hail,
That the good he doth avail.

I say unto you, you need to seek,
So the nation may finally peak.
One who for four years leads,
Not one who only for power pleads."

The Head

• • •

O this head of mine,
What do I do with thee?
I hear you a brain enshrine
That doth my thinking oversee.

All that thinking pales, though,
Compared to what must be said.
A heavy load I like to bestow
Upon you my dear head.

To carry it a fair distance
Is your true calling;
The meaning of your existence
Is to do some hauling.

To see, to smell, to smile,
To think and speak—that's fine.
To carry it's really your style;
That's where you really shine.

Mahami

• • •

Went to the restaurant Chez Ghamie,
Where the flavors flow like a tsunami.
Their sandwich with pastrami
Is as good as that with salami,
The neat cuts of sashimi
Will make you taste umami.

Then is that dish Mahami,
Left a bad feel in my tummy.
Don't eat it if you are a swami,
More for the culinary ignorami,
Needs to be cut like kirigami,
From the menu of Chez Ghamie.

Printer's Devil

• • •

O you darn printer's devil,
Why are you so evil?

You've crept into our lives
Like a bee from the hives,
Stinging away at all
With unbelievable gall.
Misery you do spread,
Our days we now dread.

You turned off the lights,
Made our days nights.
Opened the greedy floodgate,
Now corruption is our fate.
Spat at the economy,
Leaving us in ignominy.

Now you've finally done it.
Of all the pranks the summit,
You messed up the brochure,
Of that we are really sure,
Making us the butt of jokes,
From all manner of blokes.

O you darn printer's devil,
You've made our lives awful!
Go back to the hell
From where you fell,
So Ghana can flourish
And our lives nourish.

Story time with Jooma

• • •

The setting sun
Brings her shuffling in,
A sign of the fun
That she is about to spin.

Stooped over her old cane,
A body aged, haggard, and worn,
Yet in her holds a spirit reign
That looks at time with scorn.

She heads for her stool,
Set like a throne in the corner
Of the courtyard, so dim and cool,
Yet welcoming and much warmer.

Flames dance off the wall,
Casting shadowy forms
That in the imagination crawl,
As anticipation swarms.

In an arc they all sit,
Eager around her stool;
Four generations they fit
In a very tight-knit pool.

Story time with Jooma
Great-Grandma dearest,
Her words an aroma
Wafting from lands farthest.

Over hills and far away,
In the streams, along rivers—
Intrigue holds all in sway
Tales that cause the shivers.

Anxious, we all await
The phrase that starts it all;
The tension does not abate,
Till the final words fall.

"Kwezi wo ndze ndzi oo,"
She calls out.
"Wo gye dzi wa ra!"
We shout out.

Ode to Fufu

• • •

A pestle pounds
Little slivers of cassava and plantain.
The impact hounds
The poor pieces in a steady campaign.
Deftly she moves
The mix between the blows,
Even as she proves
That this chore is for the pros.
A dance it is;
Then each artist knows their part—
Never a miss
For they do it with will and heart.

Nigh steam arises
From the other dance in a pot,
Meat of all sizes,
Boiling and ready for the plot;
Then soon will swim
Sumptuous balls in an aromatic soup
And, without a whim,
Go down throats in a savoring loop.
O what a treat

For the nose, palate, and soul!
Fufu, my sweet,
You make my empty being whole.

My Parched Corner

• • •

My parched corner of the earth,
A spot all cracked and brown,
The great land of my birth,
A place where I wear a crown.
I left there in a hurry,
My fortunes abroad to seek,
And in all the flurry,
To my origin not a peek.
I went over hill and vale,
Traveled the seven seas;
So finally I did prevail
A green corner to seize.
Thus began I to dig deep,
Only parched earth to reap.

Hope for Sale

• • •

Hope for sale,
100 cedis, 200 cedis!
Hope for sale.

Preach it from the pulpits;
Give it out in little bits.
Shout it out in the streets;
Pump it out with beats.
Tell about a Savior,
With the right flavor.
His blood will heal all ills,
For ailments with no pills.

Hope for sale,
100 cedis, 200 cedis!
Hope for sale.

Despair roils our land
That remains unmanned;
Darkness against light,
Makes for a long night.
The few with hands in the pot

Stay forever and ever uncaught.
The masses hunger and thirst,
Wondering who should be first.

Hope for sale,
100 cedis, 200 cedis!
Hope for sale.

Is it any wonder?
Can one even ponder
That hope is sold
So openly and bold?
That the masses clamor,
For the Lord's armor,
To stand the arrows of anguish,
So as not to languish?

Hope for sale,
100 cedis, 200 cedis!
Hope for sale.

My Motherland, My Home

• • •

Dry winds blow
Across the charred earth.
The leafless tree slow
To give birth,
The dry air pierces,
Nostrils daring to breathe,
Even as sand a haze forces
That all envelops in its sheathe.
Ghana!
My motherland!
My home!

Thunder claps,
As water flows down drains
With hardly any gaps
To prevent floods of pains.
The earth is drenched
By tears from heaven blessed.
Our thirst is quenched,
As new life is expressed.
Ghana!
My motherland!
My home!

Seasons come and go,
Like the ebb and flow
Of trips to and fro
From a place I know.
The years cannot temper,
Distance cannot soften,
The love grows deeper,
For you, I yearn often.
Ghana!
My motherland!
My home!

To Occupy Ghana on Its Second Anniversary

• • •

They looked into the sky;
Dark clouds were nigh.
Hopelessness was a high,
Soaked the country like a dye.
So their wits they did apply,
So the great odds to defy—
The demise of Ghana to deny.
Our minds they sought to occupy
With thoughts and deeds to live by
That for Ghana we must try
To give our utmost without a sigh,
For its greatness to always vie,
Prevent it from going awry.
Your efforts we glorify.
May your success multiply,
As we say to corruption a good-bye
And to good governance an aye!

The Small Things
• • •

Interlude

• • •

HE TOOK ME TO THE town square. It was early, so the square was empty. We sat on a bench perched on the side of a knoll that overlooked the square. It wasn't long before two men walked into the square. They both wore brightly colored clothing. Simultaneously, they both started talking to each other. As I watched, I made an observation—they were both talking, but neither was listening to the other. I turned toward him, wishing for an explanation, but he seemed lost in his thoughts, so I stayed silent.

Gradually more men in brightly colored clothing streamed into the square, and like the first two men, they also started talking. Each man seemed to direct his speech to all, but no one seemed to listen to another. By now, the voices had reached a din, and I could make words out. Surprisingly, all I heard were words like "black," "white," "red," "brown," and "yellow." All I heard were descriptions of color! I strained to listen closer, and over and over, all I heard were the names of colors.

Baffled, I turned to him again. His eyes were on me with a wistful smile on his face. Before I could utter a word, he said, "All they do is speak. No one listens to the other, so all they see is each other's color."

I

She said her love was free
Before she went on the spree,
Decimating his cards,
Leaving only shards
Of his trust
In the dust.

II

Der Kland deiner Stimme,
Die Berührung deiner Hand,
Diese mir die Kraft entnehmen.
Sinnlos ist mein Widerstand
Gegen diese Leidenschaft,
Die mich in Ketten hält,
Ein Gefühl ganz fabelhaft,
Eine zärtliche, sinnliche Welt.

III

You sear their soul
With words that are weightless,
Deeds that are thoughtless,
Intent that is clueless.
Is that your goal?
To kill the priceless,
Destroy the ageless,
And leave them aimless,
So as to control?

IV

Her tears,
They run in a stream
Down her sad face.
Her fears
That her only dream
Was like a broken vase.
She hears
The distant scream
Of it fading with no trace.

V

On them we were nurtured,
As from the womb we ventured.
Love and life they gushed,
As to them we were crushed,
Now the life source has turned;
Its bearer they have spurned,
Bringing tears and pain
To what was life's domain.

VI

Rising waves off fire, sweet hope
Transfixed her,
As his shadow fell
Over her bed of sweet rose petals,
Dripping with nectar.

VII

Take me in your arms;
Whisper in my ear.
Melt me with your charms,
With words of sweet cheer.

VIII

Nothing tastes the same—
Neither the pork nor the game,
The tofu nor the bacon,
The drink stirred nor shaken—
Since you've been gone.

IX

I crave the quiet
That is only broken
By the clang of our hearts
When we touch.

X

You and me,
Ecstasy is the key.
We'll open that door
To the room with no floor,
So we can float
On the joy we wrote.
Blissful!

XI

I hear the song
In the distance.
I sing along
With persistence,
Hoping the words,
Full of longing,
Will fly like birds
To her.

XII

O bourbon,
How I love thee!
You are the sun
Shinning on the sea
In which I seek
My balance
And eke
Out my essence.

XIII

This earth is all we got.
To save it we really aught,
'Cause if we mess it up,
There sure is no backup!

XIV

Leaves got blown,
Destination unknown,
Down a lonely road,

As alone he strode,
Blind to the rain
Pelting on the stain
That is his life.

XV

A loud bang,
Then a pang—
Pain and blood,
Fear in the flood.
To you a mission,
A dark tradition.
We shake our heads
At lives in shreds.

XVI

As my soul flees,
A slow release
Fear wraps,
Tightly traps
Imagination,
Destination.
Will I be fried?
Or tried?
My voice,
Rejoice?

XVII

I don't belong
With my song
In your heart,

So I depart
In my sorrow,
My soul hollow,
Yearning,
Burning,
For you.
Only you.

XVIII

See me?
See my hopes?
See my journey?
My dreams?
Where I'm headed?
Where I'm from?
Or is there a hole where empathy
Should be?

XIX

They grew slowly,
Feeding on her
Like crabs.
They reached
Distant places.
She fell ill.
Three months?
She lived
Like never before.

XX

Sing to me,
O little bird.
Sing a song of joy.
Lift me up
Over the vale
That I may see the blooms.

XXI

Little bits of you
Get stuck to me
Anytime the dew
Of what is we
Settles on what is us.
So as passion does,
It's crazy magic.
Electricity is static,
And the little bits of you,
Stick to me like glue.

XXII

Please be kind;
Let me unwind
From this world
That me hurled
Into this life.
Bitter and rife

With pain,
No gain
To a place
With grace.

XXIII

Flying to that land
Where nothing is bland;
Magic holds sway,
And they do play
Music that lifts
Souls over rifts.

XXIV

A long, drawn-out note,
Haunting—
Loneliness is what it wrote,
Forcing
One his pain to hear,
Causing
Me to shed a tear.

Epilogue
...

At the End

• • •

As the end on me weighs,
The questions will come fast.
I'll look back on my days
To dig into the fading past.
As the grim reaper nears
To nudge me on my way,
I'll take stock of my years,
Hoping I can proudly say
That I took what was bestowed,
That gift that was only mine;
Opened it up, so it flowed
Into verses as sweet as wine—
Verses of prudence, hope, and cheer;
Verses to cope with and hold dear.

www.ingramcontent.com/pod-product-compliance
Lightning Source LLC
LaVergne TN
LVHW051522070426
835507LV00023B/3252